M000197373

...IN THIS MADNESS

RUNAWAYWRITERS

Copyright © 2020 by Runawaywriters

Illustrations by Elif Esen Gökçe

WE ARE BORN IN DARKNESS;
EACH OF US JUST A BURNING CANDLE
TRYING TO FIND OUR WAY
IN THIS MADNESS

I dedicate this book to those lost in the shadows, may your light transcend all darkness

CONTENTS

BURNING

PART ONE

And we never saw each other again.
The end

My body won't stop shaking
and I can't tell if it's from the cold
anymore

There is a distance
between us
that you won't allow me
to close

your lips say
"I'm right here"
but you move
each time I come close

// LIKE TWO MAGNETS

If you're happy
if it's all been in my head
I will wire my mouth shut
and never bother you again

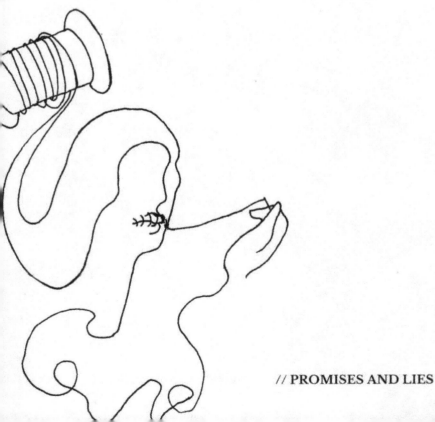

// PROMISES AND LIES

They said
I would find home in your arms
So why am I still homesick?

I hate the weak tone of my voice
when I ask you where you're going
you hate that I'm this insecure
and I hate that I have every reason to be.
We're not in love anymore, darling
we're just in pain

I was so desperate to fall in love
that I forgot to make sure
you loved me back

:

// ROOKIE MISTAKE

Mirror, mirror
on the wall
when will I be
beautiful?

// DEFINE OUTWARD BEAUTY

And soon you will tire of me,
they always do

I wrote a reminder on my phone
telling me to never talk to you again

Make sure you know they'll catch you
before you ever fall in love
for there are too many of us
laying stiff on the ground

// DIE FOR THIS LOVE

But what do you do
when that love's just lust
and that lust's not enough
anymore?

I binned the flowers you gave me
I don't know why you still try
I will never go back to you, darling
and flowers won't change my mind.
You need to walk away from me,
I am now your past.
We are just like the flowers -
nothing ever lasts

// WILTED LOVE

My angel
there are days that go by where emptiness
is a common theme
and every song
that plays
on the radio
falls victim to melancholia.
And there are nights
where my eyes have been red,
not from crying
but from the inability to sleep
so that I may reach another day.
And it's the mornings
where I could swear to God
you were right there beside me
without need to open my eyes;
feeling your warmth,
your gentle stirring

the rise and fall of your chest...
like my own heartbeat,
feeling you
because I know your rhythms so well,
they are the worst
those unforgiving mornings
where I am forced to relearn
what I already know

And it breaks my heart
that the only time
I get to hear your voice
is in the figments of my imagination

// YOU COME TO ME IN DREAMS

And I didn't
realise
how
hard
I fell
until
I tried
to get
back up

// WHEN LOVE STRIKES

It started as a love song
...and ended in a prayer

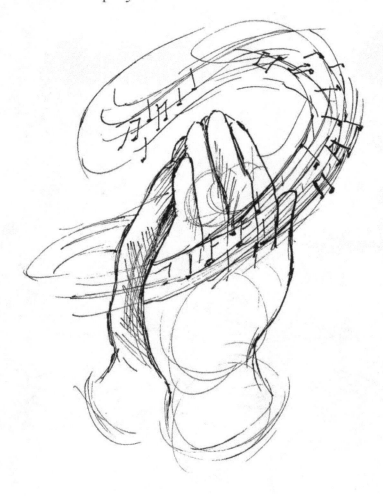

// FATHER CAN YOU HEAR ME?

When you left
I didn't think I'd ever see you again

but you visit me
every night
in my sleep

I don't hate you, darling,
I just feel sad for us

It was a one way love;
NO RETURNS

Loving you was as strange as
waking up in the middle of the night -
something always felt unfinished

Anyone want to swap hearts?
Mine is making me sick

Your eyes are black pools
guarded by signs that read
"do not swim"
It is such a shame
that love is blind

// DROWNING IN NOTHING

this delicate gift given to us -
ruined.
Your careless fingers
upon the wrapping
completely
ripped
it
apart

Are you allergic to love
or is it just me?

I spent my life savings
on your pipe dreams
of us
I went bankrupt
trying to keep us afloat
you sold me chained up promises
that weren't mine to hold on to
and now we have nothing left for us to show

// DON'T PROMISE ME THE WORLD, I'LL BELIEVE YOU

Love is kind
and you were not

I don't need you
to submerge me
in your dark shadow
to know
your sun
has set on me

Months of anger
and all you have to do
is click your fingers
and I fall to my knees

You didn't even have to love me,
you just had to be there

You move to the beat of your own drum
and my feet keep missing the steps

Oh darling,
we lost connection
long before
the phone died

// THE NUMBER YOU HAVE CALLED IS UNAVAILABLE

And I wonder
why
the tide
rolls back
afraid
to touch
the shore.
When did
the roaring
ocean
become
so distant
and demure?

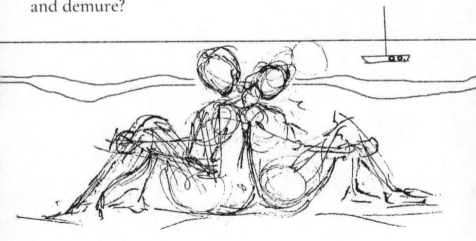

// EVERYTHING'S CHANGED

Do not be alarmed by my poetry;
they are not all about you

// THEY ARE ABOUT ME

ENGULFING

You made me realise
not all stars
are in the sky

// LIKE FIREFLIES

My heart sees happier days
each time you come around

// SO STAY

I remember the night we danced with the stars.
You held me and I saw magnolias bloom in your
eyes. I made you swear that you would dance with
me like this until our hair turned white.
"Keep this moment safe, won't you?"
You spun me out into the world and back again;
our bodies swaying like grass in a cool breeze. How
was it that there wasn't any music, yet our feet
didn't miss a beat?

// YOU MAKE ME BELIEVE IN FAIRYTALES

Put a funnel to my lips
and pour your sweet love in
I want to savour every drop

// YOU FILL ME UP

And you lay there
like a perfect reflection
of how all my mornings should be

// YOU FIT SO PERFECTLY IN THE FRAME OF MY LIFE

"I wish you were my first love," she looked at him
longingly, clutching at her arms to cover the
wounds past lovers had left on her skin. He pulled
her in close and mumbled gently into her hair.
"I'd rather be your last."

The longest journeys
always seem to have
you
at the end of them

// MEET ME HALF WAY

And it was so hard to breathe around you
when you were so intent
on taking my breath away

Your brown eyes are underrated
they speak words and tell truths -
they are the headlights of your soul;
there is no end nor beginning
to their perpetual depths
and I am lost
in rich tones of mahogany
I am lost
without desire to be found

// SEE INTO MY SOUL

When I hold you
I hold everything
I hope to never lose

That was the beauty of it, I think,
how easily we could find comfort
in the warm arms of our silence

// YOU MAKE IT SO EASY

How do I slide in "I'm in love with you"
in a normal conversation?
How do I tell you that butterflies tap dance
in the pit of my stomach every time your hand
falls to the small of my back?

// I AM INARTICULATE AROUND YOU

I knew I loved you before I met you
because I've been waiting for you my whole life

When we walk
I just want
to hold your hand.
If I'm lucky
they'll sporadically
brush together
from the misplace
steps of our feet

// CLUMSY IN LOVE

I wondered what it would be like to kiss you,
if your candy mouth would melt on mine.
I get a sugar rush just at the thought

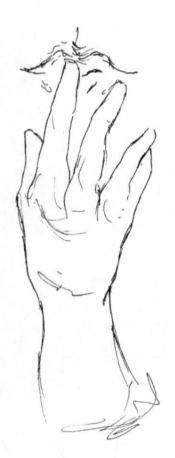

// I THINK YOU'RE SWEET

It's like there are angels in your lungs
weaving together the melody of your voice
that has become the anthem of my mornings,
the greatest hits of my nights
and the very soundtrack to my life

// I KEEP YOU ON REPEAT

Educate me on this love
I have so much to learn

// MY BESPOKE LOVE DEGREE

You kiss the nectar from my lips;
a petal soft friction
that took several missed chances
and a Nina Simone song
to get us here.
It's a sweetly scented spring afternoon
we are sat upon a tartan blanket
surrounded by daisies
my fingers are entangled in your hair
and I can taste the cherry tomatoes
fresh on your tongue

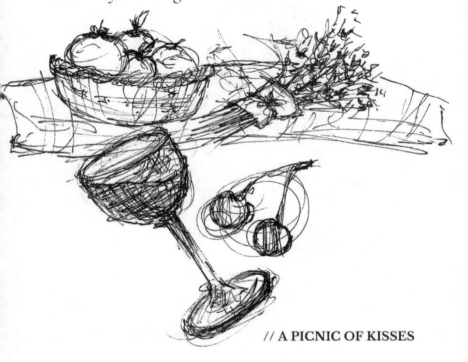

// A PICNIC OF KISSES

Be delicate
with this love
it is awfully fragile
it is our baby
and it is our duty
to keep it alive

// PARENTS TO THIS WILD CHILD "LOVE"

When I am feeling anxious
I chant your name
to settle the goosebumps on my skin
to loosen the lump in my throat
to regulate the beating of my heart
I chant your name
and feel my fists unclench
my jaw relax
and my vision clear
You have shown me a love
so spectacular
shooting stars make wishes on it
I chant your name
like it's the answer
to an equation
mathematicians have been stumped on
for decades
you have been there for me
my love
in chaos and in light
in ways you couldn't possibly imagine

// YOUR EARS MUST BE BURNING

I don't want to be
like the sun and the moon
who keep missing each other.
I want to be like the sea
and the shore -
never too far apart

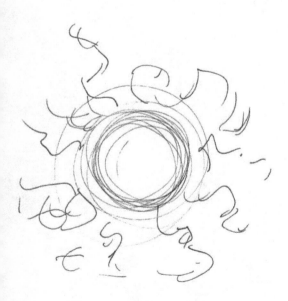

// YOU'RE NEVER REALLY GONE IF YOU ALWAYS COME BACK

I loved you once
and that was enough
to feel the current
running from your fingertips
through my whole body.
I was a robot before I met you
but now I have come to life.
You see the static tousle my hair
and now I know what it means
when they say that love is electric.

You were afraid to touch me before
but our bodies are magnets
compelling yours to mine
and we are just two crescent moons
joined together and yet still able
to make a perfect whole.
We are twin flames
thriving in the wind

I loved you once
and that was enough
for you to see
that you didn't need to look back
to know that I would always be there.

Your hand in mine
is one of the sweetest acts
that strips me down
to my core.
Body to body
I can feel the warmth of your blood
pulsating against my skin.
I loved you once
and that was enough.
We were enough

You drew back the curtains
on this love
you let our light shine in

// YOU BRING THE WARMTH OF THE SUN INSIDE

Can I be the wind
that grazes your cheek
that dances on your smile
that makes you go weak?

Can I be the wind
that propels you forward
that swirls in your lungs
that keeps you alive?

It is intoxicating
how you seep into my bloodstream
and turn poison into honey

// MY BLOOD TYPE IS U

I don't know where we're going
and I didn't pack very much
just a backpack of *I love yous*
And a prayer that it's enough

// I TRAVEL LIGHT

The ocean kisses your feet
she is as in awe of you as I am
she pulls back
and your feet sink deeper into the sand;
a surrendering of your heart
let this love be purified by the salty air
but know that to love her
is to keep her wild

// SHE PROMISES FREEDOM IN HER WAKE

GUIDING

And I hope you find
what you so crave

Strong are those who have been in love
and live to tell the tale

Lost girl
let me find you

Wake up
from your sad stupor
and remember
you can't nourish the garden
in your chest
with wine and the tar
from your cigarettes

// YOUR EYES ARE OPEN BUT ARE YOU AWAKE?

I dropped everything and ran
whizzing past trees in a blurry haze
tears flying in a flustered haste
I hadn't even gotten very far
before I realised that the only thing
I was running from was myself

// YOU CAN'T RUN FROM YOURSELF TO FIND YOURSELF

You do not love me
and that's okay -
it was a loss I was prepared for
sat sunken in the sand
I watch the waves crash and release
crash and release
...crash
and release.
It looked a lot like healing
and it felt like a never-ending cycle

// THE EBB AND FLOW OF REDEMPTION

I don't care who I lose anymore,
I just can't lose myself

Free yourself
from their barbed wire narratives
rip apart the stiff metal with your teeth
show them that you've gone through some changes
show them what it means to break free

// I DON'T LIVE IN CAGES ANYMORE

You cannot find the love you seek
if you are always looking down

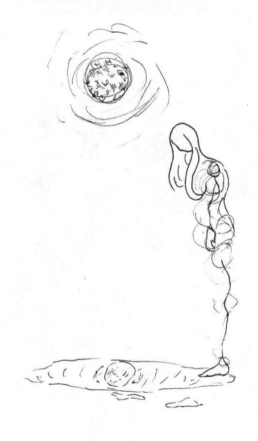

// YOU NEED TO LOOK WITHIN

It is morning
and the birds are singing
asking if you will be kinder
to yourself today

// THIS BIRD'S SONG IS ALL ABOUT YOU

Not giving up
just letting go

Didn't you tell me once
to stop resisting against the stream
to let go and be guided
to where I need to be?

// FALL BACK AND TRUST THE WINDS OF DESTINY

Repeat:
I will not waste time
pouring love into anything
that does not first start with me

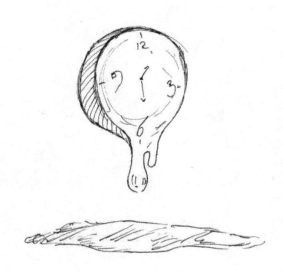

// DRINK UP LOVE, YOU HAVE BEEN PARCHED FOR A LONG
TIME

You're like a starless sky
over these urban streets
no one knows of the galaxies
you hide beneath your skin

// LIGHT ALWAYS COMES FROM WITHIN

And if you, like me,
are looking for some kind of sign
here it is

On your darkest days
remember
you have wings

She looks at you
from her spindly branch
pretty little thing.
Her head is cocked to one side
you smile from your window
she blinks
and in a further moment
she is gone
reminding you that sometimes
beauty is merely meant to be observed

// NOT EVERYTHING IS MEANT FOR KEEPS

Promise me
by sunrise
you will try to begin again

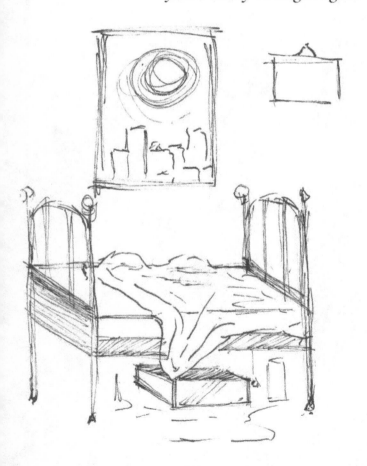

// GETTING OUT OF BED IS A TRIUMPH

You got up this morning
picked out strength
from your wardrobe
and pulled it over you
like armour

bravery allowed you
to step outside
into the light
for the first time since
your sufferings

the universe
is so proud of you
even the flowers
bow at your feet

// I WISH YOU KNEW HOW EXTRAORDINARY YOU ARE

I used to leave the candle burning for you,
now I illuminate the darkness on my own

// I AM MY OWN GUIDING LIGHT

The universe is showing me
another destiny
and
it isn't you

The sun will meet you
at 6:53 in the morning
she will lead by example
showing you
exactly how
to rise again

I hope you find that Oscar-worthy love story
I hope you find it with yourself

// AND THE AWARD GOES TO...

You do not have to smile
if you don't want to
but may I say
that when you do
it will be a grand occasion
of fireworks and glittering sparklers
to mark the day you were reacquainted
with life's gentle hand
may you walk into the light
shedding away darkness in your path
as you learn to love yourself whole
in this madness

You are a living testament
that it is possible to bleed
and still survive

I packed up all my feelings
and followed the stars
to deserted moutains -
anything I ever felt for you
I dumped over the cliff's edge.
Be gone
I said
be free

// A PURGING OF MY SOUL

Acknowledgements

I want to dedicate this book to my mother. You taught me the true meaning of love; you materialised it for me like a magic trick and I've been trying to replicate it ever since. Thank you to my father who taught me to never give up, even when things sometimes seemed impossible. If my mother taught me love, you taught me resilience.

Thank you to my siblings who helped me to see my full potential when it wasn't always visible, you believed in me, at times when it was hard to believe in myself. To my godmother, thank you for being a long-time supporter and listener of my poetry, I value you more than you know. To my godfather and my grandmother, you both inspire me tremendously with your strength and perseverance, thank you for your never-ending support. To my grandfather, you always led by example. You were a peaceful presence who taught me so much, and for that I am forever thankful.

To my dear neighbour, whom I love like family, your profound influence has helped shaped me into the person I am today. Thank you for exemplifying peace and love in 360 degrees. Thank you for being the light in my sometimes chaotic world.

Thank you to my illustrator, Elif, your hard work and creativity helped bring these words to life. I appreciate you.

To all my good friends, thank you for being a source of positivity and warmth. To those who believed in my process, who were patient when it came to reading and re-reading over my poetry; your support, love and gentleness hasn't gone unnoticed and for that I am eternally grateful. And most importantly I'd like to thank the Almighty Father for guiding me through this beautiful madness, through You anything is possible.

About the author

Runawaywriters is a London-based poet who writes as a way to understand the world around her. As a lover of adventure, the ocean and making human connections, Runawaywriters also spends time soul-searching and travelling to add more zest to her writing. She is fascinated by the colours, contrasts, perspectives and the relationship between culture and lifestyle. Find more of her words on Instagram @runawaywriters.